Children's Poems and Ilustrations:

Rural Appalachia and Family

David Thompson

Order this book online at www.trafford.com
or email orders@trafford.com

Most Trafford titles are also available at major online book retailers.

Printed in the United States of America.

ISBN: 978-1-4669-9078-4 (sc)
       978-1-4669-9079-1 (e)

Trafford rev. 1/23/2014

 www.trafford.com

North America & international
toll-free: 1 888 232 4444 (USA & Canada)
fax: 812 355 4082

$\mathscr{I}$NTRODUCTION

The following poems were written primarily for children,
although adults may find them of interest.
The poems reflect the Appalachian culture, influence and the hard times
that once existed and still do to some extent.
The poems are about a growing up experience of rural life in Appalachia.

CONTENTS

EMORIES

Down the backroad where we walked
Are some memories that help us talk

There was a shade by the swimming hole
The things we did cannot be told

The fish we caught on the river bank
Made us happy with all our pranks

The songs we sang while some baptized
Were about real truth not disguised

The quicksand bubbling from the ground
Made us look for the bubbling sound

The sycamore trees as they stood tall
Caused contemplation of things and all

O those times on the old backroad
Now help us carry the heavy load

$\mathscr{D}$AVID'S FAMILY LIFE

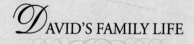

David was born on Little Larrel
Up Mud River with its sorrow

The last of twelve born for tomorrow
All could garden and could harrow

Before long they moved to a place
That was a home filled with grace

Joy and suffering could be traced
Each helped out with what they faced

Older ones looked out for the small
For our mother made us all stand tall

All were helped if one should fall
At other times we had a ball

Not all was pleasant outside of town
For some would often ramble around

Still there were no drinks nor gambling
All were secure in their rambling

David's Family Life

Birth Place

Where Born

Hill

School House Church

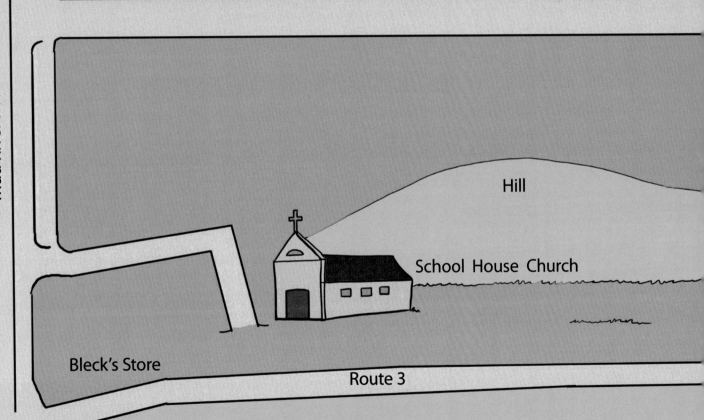

Mud River

Mud River Road

Bleck's Store

Route 3

3

MY APPALACHIAN MOTHER

My mother was as hard as nails
She was a Mom who never failed

She tried to protect her own
She made sure we were safe at home

She rarely cried unless one died
She was a Mom we could confide

She put out wash most every Monday
And cooked special food just for Sunday

She could out work any man
And was always willing to give a hand

O I know, she had her faults
But she made this life fit like a bolt

OUR FOUR GARDENS

We grew four gardens to survive
One was for corn and it did thrive

Another was cabbage, beets and tomatoes
Another with green beans and potatoes

The sweet potato garden was quite a place
Which soon was gone without a trace

All these gardens helped make us strong
And made us feel that we belonged

Old Road

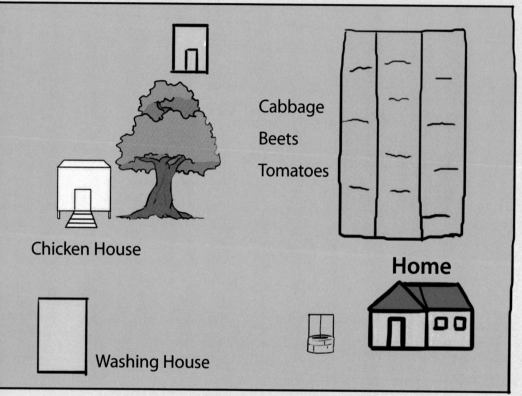

Cabbage

Beets

Tomatoes

Chicken House

Washing House

Home

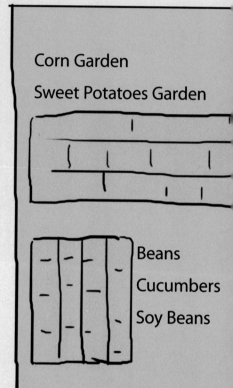

Corn Garden

Sweet Potatoes Garden

Beans

Cucumbers

Soy Beans

RT3

creek

A Farm

Summer Drought and Getting Water as Children

At summer's height our well went dry
There were no clouds from the sky

But a neighbor's well was not shy
Nor would our neighbor let us buy

Our neighbor lived a half mile away
She shared her well and turned our gray

For four long weeks to summers end
We'd pull the wagon in summer wind

My sister and I would make the round
And haul the water where it was found

Two churns of water in our red wagon
Were pulled home and were dragging

In the early morning was our task
To bring home water which did not last

At evening time we'd do the same
A water's edge was never gained

We hauled water along the road
Although hot with a heavy load

I would pull, my sister would hold
We had to scurry, we dare not fold

Hauling Water

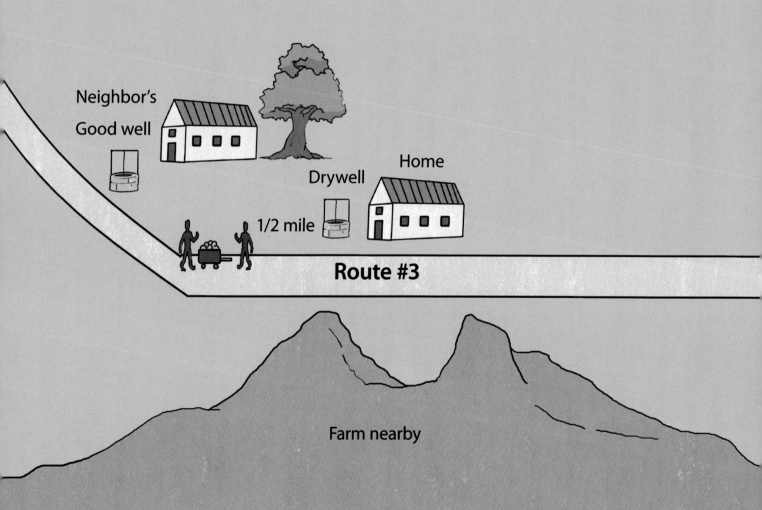

Neighbor's Good well

Drywell

Home

1/2 mile

Route #3

Farm nearby

N GRANDMA'S PORCH

On Grandma's porch I watched her rock
She lived on a hill at the end of the block

The things I saw were a wonderful lot
It was a place where the people flocked

Horseshoes were played in the yard plot
While others talked about what - not

Near the house the road to the farm
Where my Grandpa worked near his barn

He'd milk the cows and repair the sled
He worked that way until he was dead

Not a block away was the County Seat
Where the Court drew people not so neat

On the Courthouse lawn the boys would play
Until the Sheriff would chase them away

I could also see all the Church steeples
And see my friends as religious people

The stores and taverns could not be seen
Still, the Main Street was quite a scene

Horns were honked when sports teams won
And speed past Grandma's just for fun

Aunts and Uncles would visit and talk
Cousins and friends were part of the folk

O things were good on Grandma's porch
And the laughter was a like fiery torch

RATS AND SPIDERS

Rats and spiders came out at night
Rats would run rafters just for spite
They'd run around until day light
Then go elsewhere to pick a fight

The spiders were black, golden, and brown
One kept the safest distance to be found
At times they'd crawl on beds and around
And if one's bitten one could be bound

One must take care with rats and spiders
They are unlike the friendly otter
Else you'd be treated like some fodder
You could end up their bread and butter

$\mathcal{M}$Y BROTHER RAY WALKED THE LINE

My brother Ray walked the line
Among the hills and through the pines

Each time he walked, he'd look for snakes
Which he would kill for mercies sake

Rattlers were most dangerous of all
He'd kill a big one and did not fall

He loved the work in the oil field
And making sure no oil was spilled

Brother Ray walking Oil Pipe Line

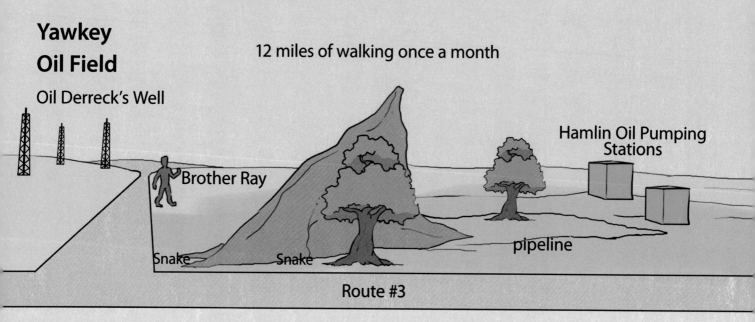

Yawkey Oil Field

Oil Derreck's Well

12 miles of walking once a month

Brother Ray

Snake

Snake

Hamlin Oil Pumping Stations

pipeline

Route #3

oil

COPPERHEADS AND RATTLERS ARE ALL AROUND

Copperheads and Rattlers are all around

But Rattlers make the rattling sound

In the country or in the town

Or walking line along the ground

One hears and looks for any found

One can also use one's hound

When snakes are found, one should pound

It isn't enough to tie and bound

Copperheads and Rattlers are all around

$\mathcal{N}$EIGHBOR: FARMER JOE

Farmer Joe was a great friend

He'd see me and let me in

He'd milk the cows and would send

He'd hoe gardens, then hogs attend

He'd work the horses to days end

He'd plant tobacco with a back bend

He'd cut mine props for business kin

He's go fishing in rain and wind

That farmer Joe was a real blend

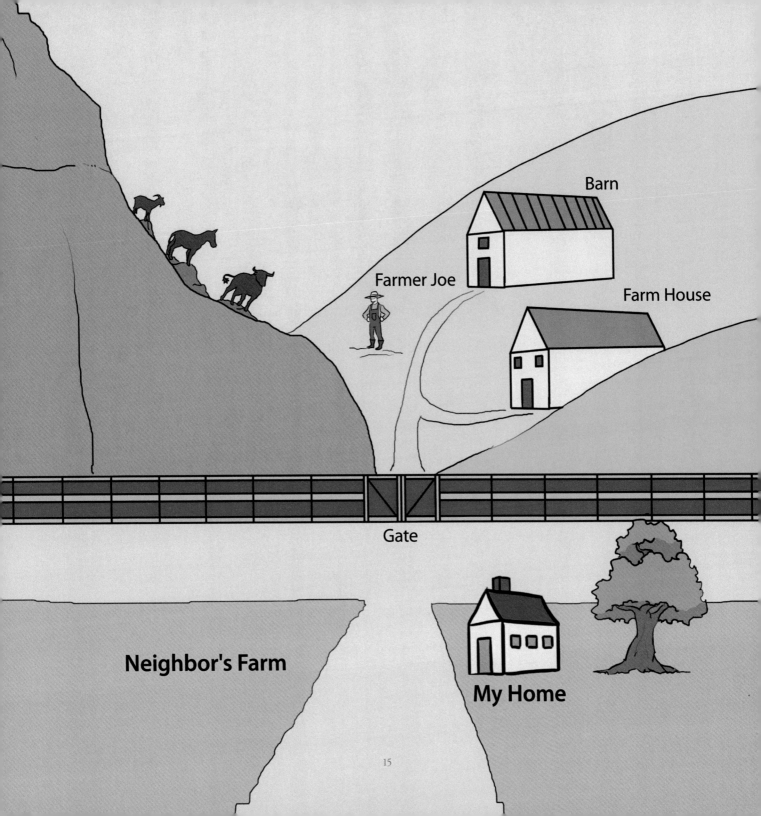

Barn

Farm House

Farmer Joe

Gate

Neighbor's Farm

My Home

15

PINKY

Pinky's name was not for real

Her red face and brown hair thrilled

She was full of fun just standing still

She could out run boys up any hill

Yet our Pinky was never shrill

She paid her part on any bill

A natural athlete with great skill

She liked all and loved to mill

She was strong with such a will

And as a farm girl she could till

WE BATHED IN A TUB FROM RAIN WATER

In the summer time with the season dry
We could not bath though we may try

Water was bad from the coal mines
In this season we could not but pine

We caught rain water in wash tubs
So once a week we could be scrubbed

It was a sight with a tub brought in
And buckets of water poured in the tin

My mother washed my sister and me
While siblings watched with great glee

Siblings also used rain water
But outside for they were older

We all used the same old tub
To scrub our feet and rub, rub, rub

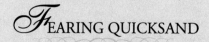EARING QUICKSAND

Quicksand is common along Mud River
And getting near can make one shiver

A watery sand along river and bank
Preys on victims who may play pranks

A horse can sink and be lost
No way to save nor to boast

No signs are out, one must watch
For large bubbles one can't catch

I still have fear where I have walked
While other laughed and just talked

*M*Y AUNT JENNY

My Aunt Jenny was somewhat old
And stayed removed from the family fold

She did not trust what she did not know
She did not drink but she could scold

She owned a 1914 Model T Ford
She crossed the river at the ford

As wheels were tall she avoided water
She was kept safe with her butter

In weather bad or weather good
She'd cross the river to sell her food

She travelled this way to get through
As bridges around were very few

She lived up high from Mud River
She wasn't flooded nor did she shiver

I'd watch her convertible going by
A black four passenger that made me sigh

$\mathcal{M}$OUNTAIN WOMAN

In Appalachia on a mountain top
Lives my woman who makes life hop

When she talks and starts to walking
It is time to stop all of the balking

She cooks meals and makes kids mind
If they do not then she will fine

She hoes the gardens in her blue jeans
The bears dare not come near this queen

She tends the sheep and knows them all
If one should cry she knows its call

She knows the cows, they know her name
If a bull gets feisty, she's quick to tame

O I tell you, I love this woman
No one dare send an evil omen

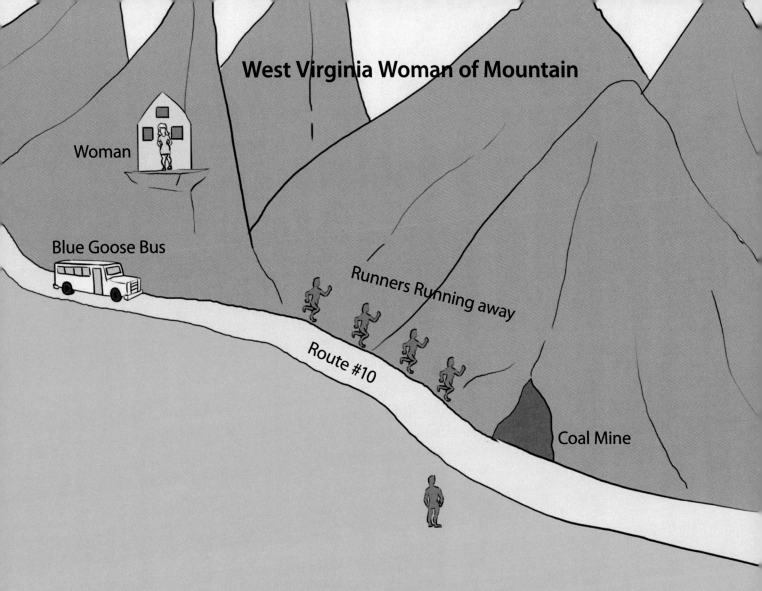

Up Charlie's Creek My Sister Lived

I

Up Charlie's Creek my sister lived
Off 34 where one could drive
10 children there did so thrive
They worked the farm to survive
Greeting all when they arrived

II

They raised chickens, hogs and corn
They started work in early morn
They seldom ever were forlorn
While milking cows that had horns
In the place they were born

III

Each day had work in its pleasure
The way they did it was a treasure
Opal's man knew how to measure
Both the work and the leisure
Which was indeed a great feature

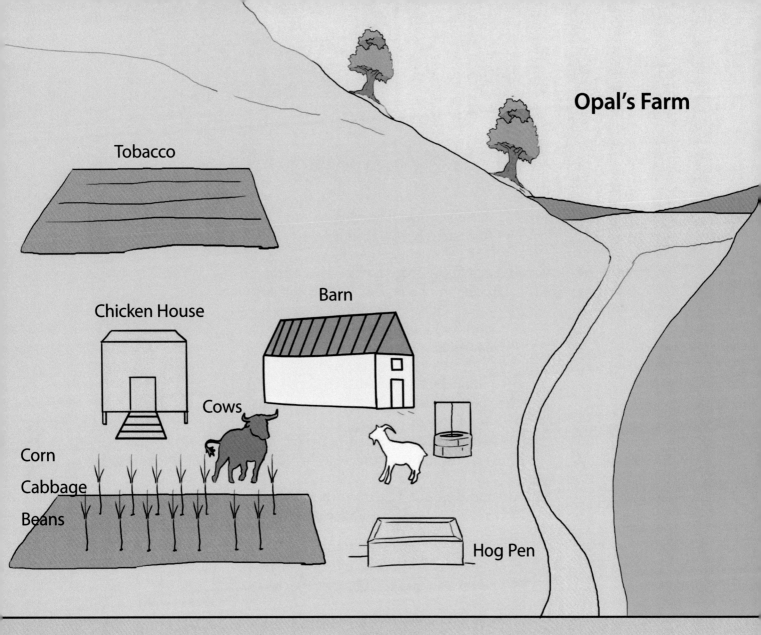

Opal's Farm

Tobacco

Chicken House

Barn

Cows

Corn

Cabbage

Beans

Hog Pen

RT. 34

A BELL CROWD

A Bell Crowd was a happy time
It seemed to make all life rhyme

Each home stored away crow bells
To celebrate marriage and its thrills

Two weeks after a couple married
A surprise visit made them scurry

Unannounced the word was spread
Get out the Bell and bring some bread

Although the couple were prepared
They did not know how well they'd fair

People would gather on their lawn
To shake the bells and have some fun

Candy was given for children to eat
While the others ran and danced a beat

Soon the happy time lost its rapture
Then bells were stored with their clapper

Bell Crowd

cars

Route 3

25

GAYONDOTTE RIVER AND COAL TRAIN RACE

The Gayondotte is a River to spot
There was at time when She was hot

Tracks at Branchland were on one side
Where coal and passengers took a ride

On the other side of the Gayondotte
Was a wide road where one could plot

Straight stretches lay along the way
While tracks and river had their sway

The River would rise at flood time
But coal continued from the mines

The boys would race to beat the train
Driving fast cars which seemed insane

On a stretch near River and train
My friend Odell would try to tame

He'd stomp the throttle to the floor
Speeding along to make a score

At one end was West Hamlin bridge
He'd tried to cross to see what gives

At times we'd beat that big steam engine
At times we'd stop or be clay pigeons

In either case we'd have our laugh
By beating death from cutting in half

Odel, Me and Paul Beating the Train

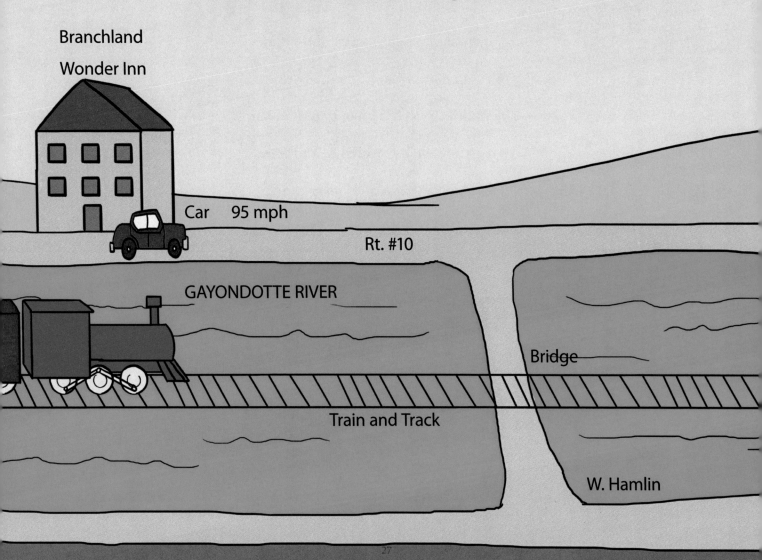

Branchland

Wonder Inn

Car   95 mph

Rt. #10

GAYONDOTTE RIVER

Bridge

Train and Track

W. Hamlin

THE OIL PUMP STATION

The Oil Pump Station ran all the time

In summer or winter, in rain or shine

The pumps moved oil like things rhyme

The storage tanks were big and fine

I'd sleep at night and never pine

I loved the sounds, they were just mine

The Station Master was very kind

He'd show me engines and their spine

Day or night was such a find

You could see all unless blind

The place gave me a peace of mind

Oil Pumping Station

Morton and Piston

Morton and Piston

Tool House

Route #3

Oil Tank

Fire Ring

side walk

Oil Tank

Fire Ring

Oil Tank

Fire Ring

Fire Bank

Fire Bank

Creek

Home

$\mathscr{S}$KIP

Skip was young with little wants

There was no desire for the Bronx

He worked in woods uprooting trunks

His one desire caused a deep lump

He loved coal mining for big humps

He'd been laid off for lack of lumps

He wanted only to do his stunt

For something else, he would not punt

My Uncle Charlie

Uncle Charlie's home sat way on top
Where one could see from any spot

His greetings were on the way to school
"Comment-telle-vous, how are you?"

He was wounded in World War I
While in France and carrying a gun

He belonged to the American Legion
He was respected throughout the region

At the Post Office he was a clerk
He'd straighten out all of the quirks

For years he taught in Sunday School
He taught pupils what they should do

He served as Mayor of our town
He was the best from all around

My Uncle Charlie was one fine man
He was always willing to give a hand

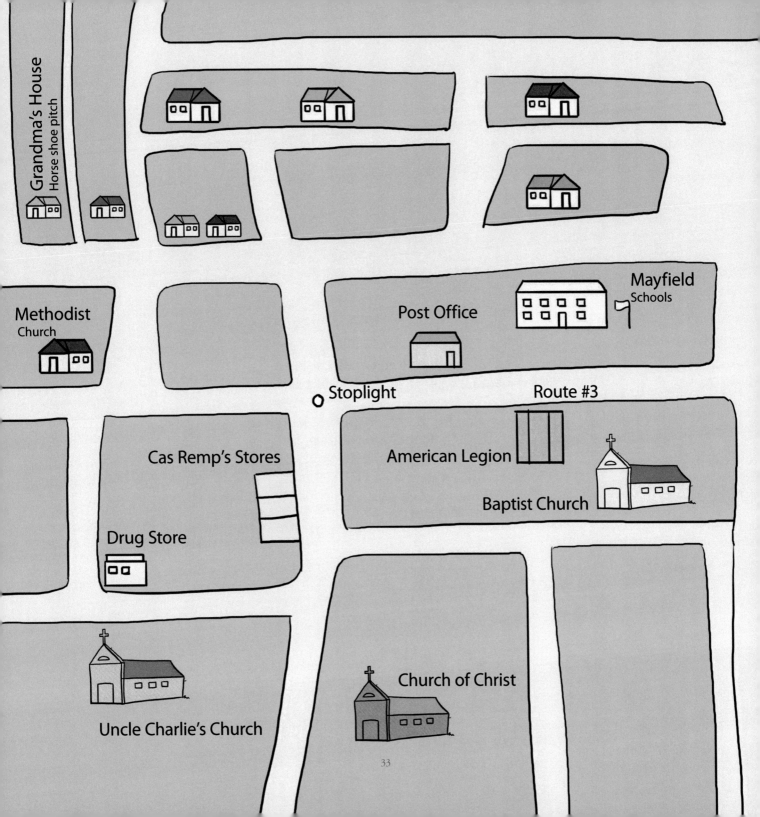

Grandma's House
Horse shoe pitch

Methodist
Church

Mayfield
Schools

Post Office

Stoplight

Route #3

Cas Remp's Stores

American Legion

Baptist Church

Drug Store

Uncle Charlie's Church

Church of Christ

33

$\mathcal{M}$Y BROTHER ROMA

My brother Roma could not see
Yet he was musical, all could agree

He played the fiddle, mandolin, and harp
And made the guitar do its part

I often hear his musical songs
Though he lays in the cold ground

Brother Roma and Guitar

Romas's Other Musical Instruments

Banjo

Harmonica

Fiddle and Bow

Mandolin

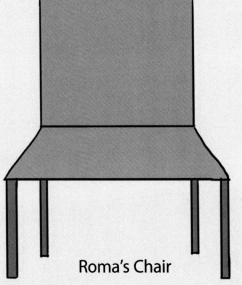

Roma's Chair

$\mathcal{M}$Y FRIEND CHARLES

My friend Charles was a real man
He was ready to give a willing hand

He was Coach of the Basketball
And really made the boys stand tall

He taught the students about his Math
In other courses guiding right paths

He taught the boys on the sports team
They thought he was a coaches dream

An outstanding leader in High School
He never made one look a fool

Basketball

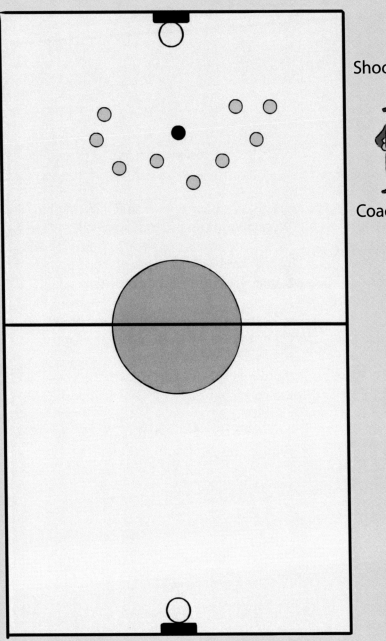

Shoot the ball

Coach Elkins

$\mathcal{T}$ENT MEETING REVIVAL

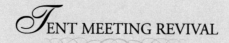

Tent Meetings of the annual revival
Were all about spiritual survival

The workers would come to set up
Some would have a money cup

They'd shout and preach far too long
They would end up with a Gospel song

Some were saved in that place
Lives were changed with no disgrace

For one week the meetings went
Then it was time to fold the tent

Revival Tent Meeting

In Town

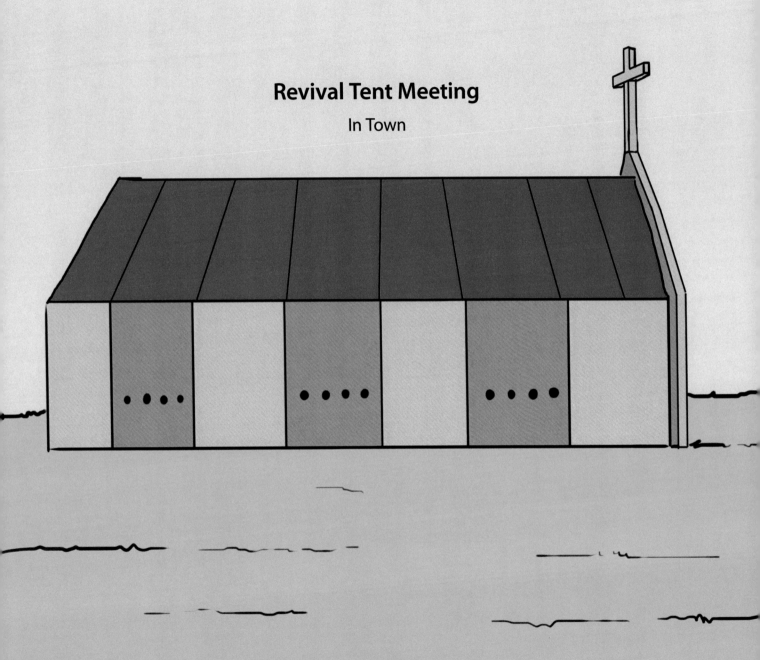

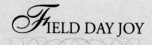FIELD DAY JOY

School Field Day was a special day

We had much fun as we played

There was no time for much to say

Events moved fast without the gray

We played games and were so gay

High Jumps were high from where we lay

Playing marbles kept some at bay

We made Ball scores come what may

The joy we had was like a sun ray

Field Day at Playing Field

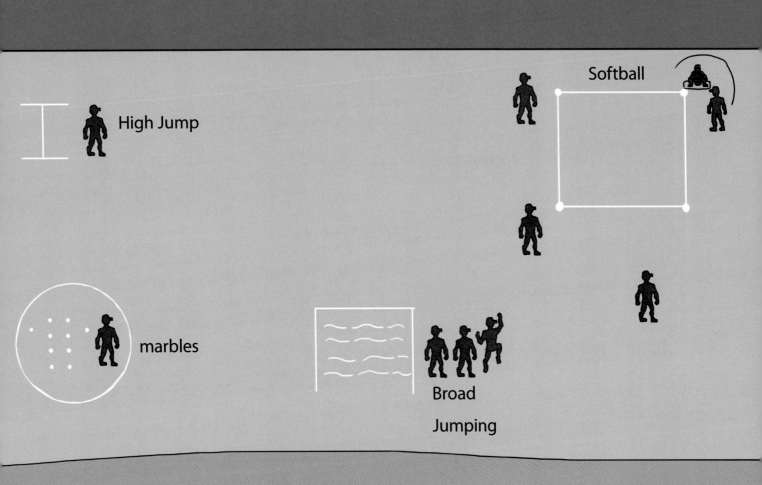

High Jump

marbles

Broad Jumping

Softball

$\mathcal{B}$IG JIM ROBERTS

Big Jim Roberts was my friend
From early childhood to the end

He was our Coach and was mine
He pushed us hard but not unkind

He was our Coach after the War
He was wounded on another shore

He was head of sports and football
At six foot three, he made calls

He taught us all to be good sports
And when losing not to retort

What a man, we loved him so
We all hated to see him go

He was strong right to the end
Still, to this day he is my friend

Ball Field

move it!

Big Jim

Bleachers

ALL DAY MEETING AND DINNER ON THE GROUND

All Day Meeting and Dinner on the Ground
Was the best of summer all around

Meetings took place at Harvey Creek Church
With such excitement that one almost burst

Classes were held for children and all
It was late summer and not quite fall

Then preaching and singing would begin
There seldom was a time to end

Especially if the Preacher got wind
But he would stop so as not to offend

Then noon-time was a great treat
There was much food so all could eat

For two quick hours we ate and played
Then began for the rest of the day

Singing and preaching could be heard
All tried to speak and hear God's Word

Stopping at four some were baptized
There was no waiting nor disguise

All went home a happy bunch
And all received more than a lunch

All Day Meeting and Dinner on the Ground

Tables

Food Table

Harvey Creek

Church

Benches

Horse Shoes

water stream

Route 34

By THE RIVER FORD

At the Mud River Ford O the things that were

Folks would gather to take a dare

The boys would skinny-dip and not care

Fishermen would forge with some wares

Boats were launched with little fear

Baptisms occurred as God was near

Such were the times as all peered

By the river for O the things that were

Mud River

Old Road

Route 3

Mud River Ford

THE WHITAKER ROCKS A PLACE TO PLAY

On Whitaker Rocks we played our games

And nothing ever was the same

Boulders and rocks would be tamed

Hiding places drew much fame

Near the rocks were great tree frames

Grapevines hanging were not for lame

We'd jump on them and take our aim

Riding back and forth without much pain

Then we'd go home with what we gained

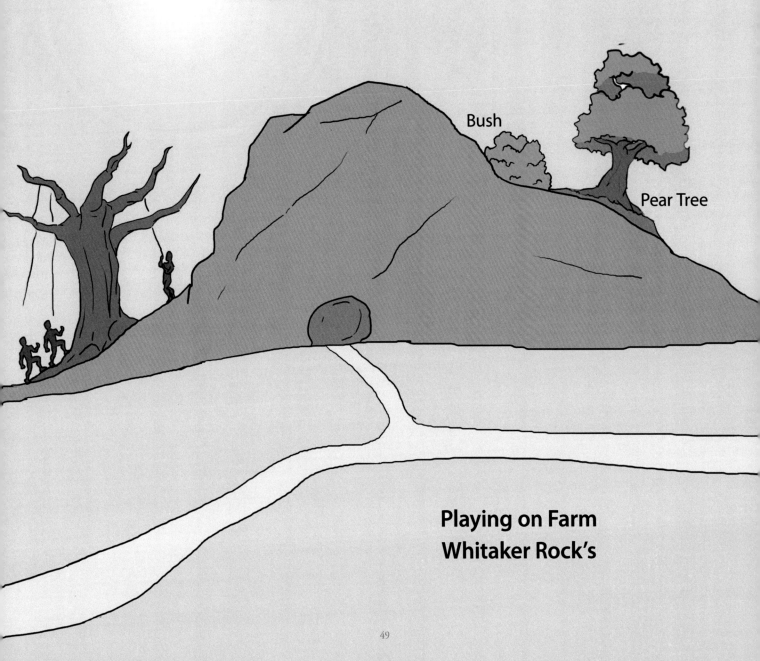

Sun

Bush

Pear Tree

**Playing on Farm
Whitaker Rock's**

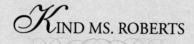KIND MS. ROBERTS

Kind Ms. Roberts was eighty five
She helped all while still alive

If some were sick, she would call
If some were weak, she was tall

If some were strong, she was weak
If some were lost, she would seek

Now she lays in her own tomb
In the place that is her room

She loved all, both young and old
She wanted all in her God's fold

Ms. Roberts Laid to Rest

Number Nine Coal

Number Nine Coal, O Number Nine Coal
It's served the people, now its too old
Many a day came forth black gold
While dead miners lay in the cold

There's some talk of returning bold
But it has served and now must fold
I can't but tell you I want to hold
Number Nine Coal, O Number Nine Coal

A MEMORY OF THE RIVER BANK

I love to think about the old tree
On the river bank where life agreed
Under the sycamore where I was free
With great beauty around to see

The old green river gave me glee
There I sat with just me
With a fishing pole near my lee
Life for me did so agree

But now I'm old that time has gone
As is my home where I belonged
Yet I remember and I've longed
Where I caught fish and sang songs

REMEMBERING A TIME IN LOGAN COUNTY

Things of Logan I so remember
In those cold days of November

I remember the lone bleak place
Yet a people filled with grace

I remember eating hot dogs
From the window watching fog

I remember the old bus station
And the drinkers expressing passion

I remember feeling right at home
And black coal that stood alone

I remember just how it was
And a few who liked to fuss

I remember old Logan County
And a people really country

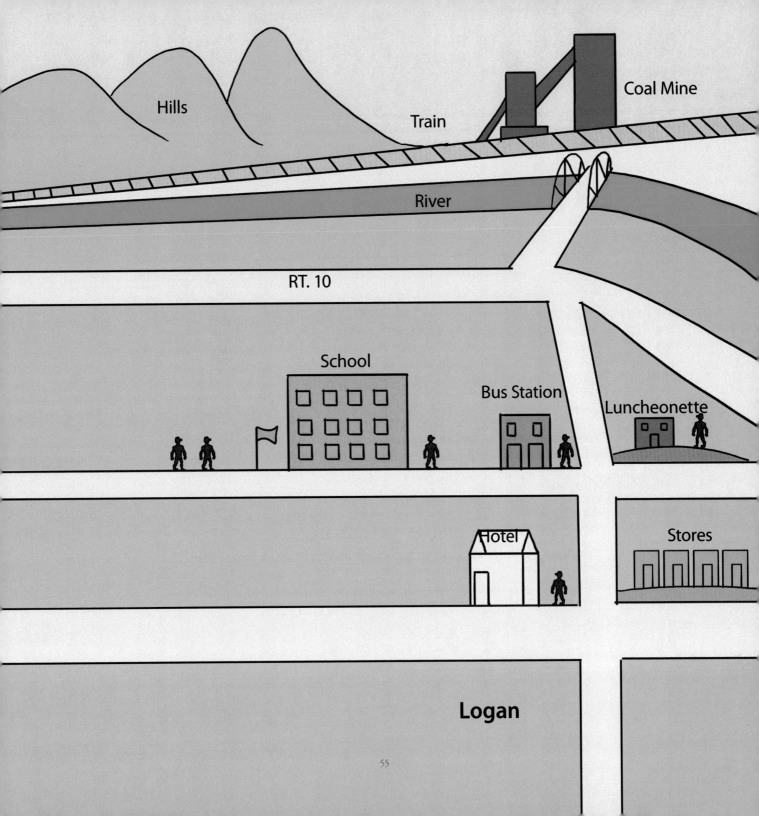

Hills

Coal Mine

Train

River

RT. 10

School

Bus Station

Luncheonette

Hotel

Stores

Logan

55

ℳY DAD AND THE PEAR TREE EXPERIENCE

The pear tree experience with me and Dad
Most always helps me when I am sad

My Dad and me went to our farm
Not far from home but it had charm

The farm had meadows, three in all
With three pear trees, big and tall

One summer day we picked and picked
With three burlap sacks that did the trick

Then we were tired and I was real hot
My Dad said, "Let's rest in this cool spot."

Near the trees at the top of a hill
Spring water flowed like a small mill

Dad said, "Let's drink from the spring."
And it was so good I wanted to sing

A good neighbor hauled our pears to town
The best tasting pears from all around

I'll never forget that happy day
Dad helping me in my growing way

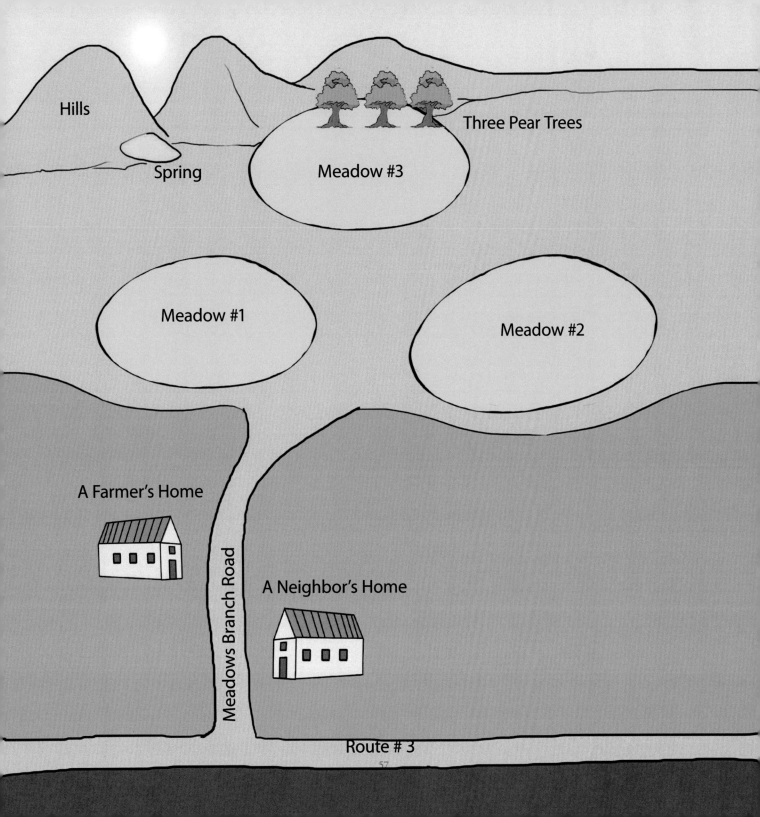

Hills

Spring

Three Pear Trees

Meadow #3

Meadow #1

Meadow #2

A Farmer's Home

Meadows Branch Road

A Neighbor's Home

Route # 3

Printed in the United States
By Bookmasters